7600 sw 29 st
Mercer Island
98040

Meet the characters

The Yogi Petz™

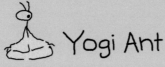 Yogi Ant

 Yogi Mouse

 Yogi Turtle

 Yogi Elephant

 Yogi Raccoon

 Yogi Rabbit

 Yogi Firefly

 Yogi Chameleon

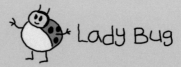 Lady Bug

To meet and find out more about the cast visit:
www.sketchesinstillness.com

Sketches in Stillness

Volume 2

A wise blind old man once said:
"There is a light in you that existed before
the sun was created and that will exist long
after the sun is no more." ~Yogi Turtle

you are the light

"We are not human beings having a spiritual experience.
We are spiritual beings seemingly having a human experience."

~ Pierre Teilhard de Chardin

Somebody sometime, disapproved of yourself
and you started disapproving of yourself...

We see the world through a muddy vail...

"We never really meet each other,
we mostly meet the past. Caught in our own
views of the world, opinions, judgments,
(our parent's view of the world)
we rarely are present to the people
we meet."

~Francois

" We only see what we think."

Love is our true nature.

"No one is born hating another person
because of the color of his skin,
or his background, or his religion."
~ Nelson Mandela

We stress because we think
we are little sunbeams separated from the sun (our source)
and from one another.

"There is a light in you that nothing can extinguish."

~ François

No matter how covered the light
Seems to be...

Fear

Sadness

Anger

Guilt

... The sun always
Shines behind the clouds.
you are the sun . ~ Yogi Firefly

We are all illuminated by the same light...

"The Lamps are different but the Light is the same."

~ Rumi

"In a moment of no Thoughts, of silence, we can realize our Oneness."
~ Francois

"There is nothing you need to carry
that isn't light."

~Yogi Firefly

" you came on the earth with nothing
you will leave the earth with nothing,
don't sweat over stuff, keep it light ! :)"

~Francois

"The past is not clinging to you;
you are clinging to the past.
Once you are not clinging, the past
simply evaporates."

~Osho

"Don't let yesterday use up too much of today."
~Cherokee Indian Proverb

"It is amazing the energy we spend
holding on to our past fears in order to
predict our future misery. We'd rather
be afraid and in control, than to dare
fully enjoy the present moment."

~ François

"your reaction to an event
can hurt you more than
the actual event."

~Francois

"Worrying is using your imagination
to create something you do not want."
~Abraham Hicks

"The voice in your head is something you are watching, it's not something that you are ...

As you are watching, see if what that voice is saying is really helpful or is it just a neurotic voice talking in your head." ~ Michael Singer

You are not your thoughts unless you actually choose them.
No need to dwell on them, act on them, fight with them
or try to avoid them. Take notice and let them go.
~John Shearer, Mindfulness Coach

"Don't take your abusive mental self talk personally,
don't cling to it, let it loose, let it flow by like
clouds in the sky."

~ Yogi Ant

You are not the clouds,
you are the sky...

"Don't try to stop your anxious thoughts
that come into your mind, let them come in,
and let them go out, they won't stay long
if you don't hang on to them."

~ François

"Do not anticipate trouble or worry
about what may never happen,
Keep in the sunlight."
~Benjamin Franklin

Nothing can hurt you more than your unobserved thoughts.

The moment you become aware of an abusive thought, you are free from it, you become the light that is aware of the thought, you are no longer one with it.

" Who would I be without these thoughts?"
~ Byron Katie

"Whenever you observe something
without judgment, you put light on it."

~ Francois

"A moment of awareness is priceless,
it is a moment in which you can observe
clearly what thoughts prevent you
to experience peace."

~ Francois

"If we stopped seeing the world through the past,

everyone would be our valentine."

~ françois

"Love is when you look into someone's eyes
and you don't see the past,
you only see their heart."

~ François

YOUR MIND CONSTANTLY ABSORBS ALL YOUR ATTENTION, WITH ONE WORRY AFTER ANOTHER PRETENDING TO BE NECESSARY...

IT DISTRACTS YOU FROM FEELING THE PRICELESS GOODNESS PRESENT IN YOURSELF THIS VERY MOMENT !!!

TAKE A BREATH : NOTICE THE AIR GOING IN AND OUT OF YOUR LUNGS RIGHT NOW.
CAN YOU FEEL YOUR HEART BEAT THIS VERY SECOND?
CAN YOU FEEL THE MIRACLE IT IS TO BE ALIVE?

IT IS THROUGH A QUIET MIND, THAT THE LIGHT OF ETERNAL PEACE CAN SHINE INTO THIS WORLD.

"Allow your thoughts and feelings to come and go freely without judgment. Observe them without trying to stop them and watch them settle down like snow settling down at the bottom of an untouched snow globe."

~ Yogi Turtle

Be like a river...

Let your emotions flow through you
without shame, guilt or judgment.

~ François

When you observe your negative thoughts and
emotions, without judgment, without becoming
identified with them, letting them happen
with love and acceptance,
the mud of guilt and shame
will melt away.

~Yogi Firefly

Take a bath of Self acceptance, and non judgment.
Stop asking that this moment be different than
what it is. It's okay to be feeling whatever you
you are feeling this very moment. It's okay to
be exactly where you are this very moment in
your life. It is all okay right Now.

~ Yogi Firefly

"Accept, then act. Whatever the present moment contains, accept it as if you had chosen it, always work with it, not against it...

When you complain you make yourself into a victim.

Complaining is adding a rock on top of the situation

Leave the situation,
Change the situation or accept it.
All else is MADNESS."
~ Eckhart Tolle

"It is better to light a candle than to curse the darkness."

~chinese proverb

Feeling guilty that you got angry is adding another rock on top of the anger

Take a breath, observe the anger, accept it, let it go you'll do better next time...

" Just know that whatever you are feeling
inside yourself, this very moment,
is completely okay."

~ François

When you tell yourself that it's okay not to
be at peace this very moment,
then you become peaceful.

~ Yogi Turtle

" To be enlightened doesn't mean that you won't have any negative thoughts anymore, it means that even while entangled in these thoughts, you allow them to be without believing in them and they will dissolve."

françois

"if you are able to love yourself in the midst of your abusive thoughts and emotions, you will bloom, like the lotus blooms untouched by the mud."

~Yogi Firefly

"The lotus flower blooms most beautifully
from the deepest and thickest mud."
~Yogi Firefly

" Be to yourself the kindest, most loving, gentle,
unjudging friend you have ever known.
Be to yourself the love of your life."

François

At the end of the day, tell yourself gently:
"I love you, you did the best you could today,
and even if you didn't accomplish all you
had planned, I love you anyway."

~ François

What does "you are the light" mean?
The less you carry, the lighter you become ;
Lightness, joy, freedom is who you truly are.

~Yogi Firefly

"Do not seek after love, but simply remove the barriers you have built against it. "
~ Rumi

Don't seek for anyone's approval,
you've got it all in you,
just be yourself.

~ François

"All the darkness in the world
cannot extinguish the light
of a small candle."

~ St Francis

"It feels so good to be in the presence of a tree or an animal, because it has no opinion about anyone not even itself. That space of no opinion, of l♥ve, is present in everyone." ~Francois

"Gently shine your light of non-judgement
on all the shady parts of yourself and
in the process you will get acquainted
with the brightness of who you truly are."

~Yogi Turtle

"When you practice self-compassion and embrace your imperfections, the light of unconditional love will flow from you into the world." ~Francois

"What lies behind you and what lies in front of you,

Pales in comparison to what lies inside of you."
~ Ralph Waldo Emerson

"No need to look at the weather forecast today ...

... I am the sunshine of my life."
~Yogi Firefly

"A smile is the window on your face
that shows that there is light within."

~yogi Firefly

"You are responsible for the energy
you bring in the room."
~Iyanla Vanzant

" If you light a lamp for somebody,
it will also brighten your own path. "

~ Buddha

"Thousands of candles can be lit from a single candle
and the life of the candle will not be shortened.
Happiness never decreases by being shared."

~ Buddha

"We fear because we think we are ephemeral ripples on the surface of the sea; We forgot we are the eternal ocean, temporarily appearing as ripples."

François

In the depth of your being,
under the stormy surface of your mind,
there is a vast ocean of perfect peace.

What fearful thoughts need you take
little ripple, once you realize you are the eternal ocean?
Fear dissolves, love and grace is experienced and that
becomes the supply you can give to the world.

"Love is but the discovery of ourselves in others,
and the delight in the recognition."
~ Alexander Smith

Good morning little sunbeam, I am your source, the Sun. I will be handling all your problems today. I won't be needing your help, just relax, shine, and have a great day!

Once you realize you are one with your source, you shine, and that light radiates unconditionally on everyone you meet.

Let your peace shine on everyone...

"The sun shines on everyone, it doesn't make choices."

~ Snatam Kaur

Remember you are the light,
and that light ever gives of itself unconditionally...

" Even after all this time the sun
never says to the earth, "you owe me".
Just think what a love like that could do,
It lights up the whole world."
~ Hafiz

"Let me see today not what I can get,
but let me see today what I can give.
In what way can I be an instrument
in the service of peace, love and kindness."

~ Francois

"The more you give of your fruits unconditionally
The more your fruits will multiply infinitely."

~ François

"A peaceful presence speaks louder
than thousands of wise words."

~ Yogi Chameleon

"Teach by example."

~ Francois

"The feeling of not holding any thoughts about ourselves or others for just a few seconds is peace on earth."

~ François

" Be a fertile ground of peace, invite
every little seedlings around you
to bloom guiltlessly in your atmosphere
of no judgement. "

~ François

Once you realize you are the eternal ocean you have all the time in the world...

"Being with someone, listening without a clock and without anticipation of results, teaches us about love. The success of love is in the loving, it is not in the result of loving."
~ Mother Teresa

"If you judge people you have no time
to love them." ~Mother Teresa

"When you give someone time, you make space
on your daily schedule for eternity to be you.
unhurried attention is called L♥ve."

~françois

"If you get the inside right,
The outside will fall into place."
~ Eckhart Tolle

Illustrated by François Lange
to find out more about the author visit:
www.sketchesinstillness.com
www.facebook.com/sketchesinstillness

Made in the USA
Middletown, DE
10 January 2019